FUZZY I
FESTIV

BY BARBARA PRIME

TABLE OF CONTENTS

BIG POLAR TEDDY
WITH A SNOWFLAKE SWEATER

TEDDY

Materials

100g of white chunky/bulky weight yarn, small amount of yarn for embroidering face, two 12 mm (½") black buttons or safety eyes, stuffing, pair of 5 or 5.5 mm (US size 8 or 9) knitting needles, tapestry needle

Measurements

36 cm (14") tall

Gauge

18 sts and 24 rows per 10 cm (4")

If you use chunky yarn for the bear, you will want to use 5 mm needles to knit it, and make the small sweater size. If you use bulky yarn for the bear, you will want to use 5.5 mm needles and make the medium sweater size.

Legs (make 2)

Begin at sole.

Cast on 10 sts. P 1 row.
Next: k1, [m1, k1] to end. (19 sts)
  P 1 row.
Next: k4, [m1, k3] 5 tries. (24 sts)
Work 5 rows in st st.
Next: k8, [skpo] twice, [k2tog] twice, k8. (20 sts)
Next: p6, [p2tog] twice, [p2tog tbl] twice, p6. (16 sts)
Next: k7, k2tog, k7. (15 sts)
Work 3 rows in st st.
Next: k2, m1, k11, m1, k2. (17 sts)
Work 13 rows in st st.
Next: k1, [k2tog] 8 times. (9 sts)
Break off yarn. Thread end through remaining stitches, and pull tight to gather. Sew up sole and back leg seam, leaving an opening. Stuff and close opening.

Body

Begin at neck edge.

Cast on 17 stitches. P 1 row.
Next: k1, [m1,k1] to end. (33 sts)

Work 5 rows in st st.
Next: [k8, m1] twice, k1, [m1, k8] twice. (37 sts)
Work 7 rows in st st.
Next: k17, m1, k3, m1, k17. (39 sts)
Work 5 rows in st st.
Next: k4, m1, k1, m1, k29, m1, k1, m1, k4. (43 sts) P 1 row.
Next: k18, skpo, k3, k2tog, k18. (41 sts)
Work 3 rows in st st.
Next: k17, skpo, k3, k2tog, k17. (39 sts)
Work 3 rows in st st.
Next: k1, [k2tog] 17 times. (20 sts)
  P 1 row.
Next: [k2tog] to end. (10 sts)
Break off yarn. Thread end through remaining stitches, and pull tight to gather. Sew up back seam to neck edge (leaving neck edge open). Stuff.

Right arm

Begin at paw tip.

Cast on 7 stitches. P 1 row.
Next: k1, [m1, k1] to end. (13 sts)
  P 1 row.
Next: k1, [k1, m1, k2] 4 times. (17 sts)
Work 5 rows in st st.
Next: k1, [skpo] twice, k1, [k2tog] twice, k7. (13 sts)
Work 5 rows in st st.
Next: k7, [m1, k3] twice. (15 sts)
Work 11 rows in st st.
Next: k1, [k2tog] 7 times. (8 sts)
Break off yarn. Thread end through remaining stitches, and pull tight to gather. Sew up seam, leaving an opening. Stuff and close opening.

Left arm

Begin at paw tip.

Cast on 7 stitches. P 1 row.
Next: k1, [m1, k1] to end. (13 sts)
  P 1 row.
Next: k1, [k1, m1, k2] 4 times. (17 sts)
Work 5 rows in st st.
Next: k7, [skpo] twice, k1, [k2tog] twice, k1. (13 sts)

Work 5 rows in st st.
Next: [k3, m1] twice, k7. (15 sts)
Work 11 rows in st st.
Next: k1, [k2tog] 7 times. (8 sts)

Break off yarn. Thread end through remaining stitches, and pull tight to gather. Sew up seam, leaving an opening. Stuff and close opening.

Head

Begin at back of head.

Cast on 8 sts. P 1 row.
Next: k1, [m1, k1] to end. (15 sts)
  P 1 row.
Next: k1, [m1, k1] to end. (29 sts)
Work 3 rows in st st.
Next: [k3, m1] 3 times, k11, [m1, k3] 3 times. (35 sts)
Work 13 rows in st st.
Next: k8, [k2tog] twice, k11, [skpo] twice, k8. (31 sts) P 1 row.
Next: k1, [k2tog] 6 times, k5, [skpo] 6 times, k1. (19 sts)
Work 5 rows in st st.
Next: k1, [k2tog] to end. (10 sts)

Break off yarn. Thread end through remaining stitches, and pull tight to gather. If using safety eyes, attach them to head now. Sew up seam, leaving an opening. Stuff and close opening. Make sure to put extra stuffing in the nose to make it stick out.

Ears (make 2)

Start at ear tip.

Cast on 6 sts. K 1 row.
Next: k1, m1, k4, m1, k1. (8 sts) K 1 row.
Next: k1, m1, k6, m1, k1. (10 sts)
Work in garter stitch for 5 rows.
Next: Cast off.

Cast-off edge will be attached to head.

Finishing

Sew button eyes in place (or embroider eyes with black yarn if the toy is for a very young child). With length of yarn, embroider nose and mouth. Sew ears in place on head. Sew head securely to the open neck edge of body. Thread a length of yarn through left arm about 1 cm from top, thread yarn through body at shoulder position, then thread yarn through right arm. Thread yarn through body again, and then the left arm and pull tight (see diagram in the tip on p. 26). Repeat so yarn passes through each arm 3-4 times. Pull yarn tight so arms are secure, then fasten off yarn. Attach legs at lower edge of body in the same way as the arms.

SWEATER

Materials

50g of worsted weight yarn, pair of 4 or 4.5 mm (US size 6 or 7) knitting needles, set of four 4 or 4.5 mm dpns, tapestry/darning needle, scrap yarn

Measurements

25-28 cm (10") around, 10-12 cm (4-4¾") long

Gauge

22 sts and 32 rows per 10 cm (4")

For small size, use 4 mm needles. For medium size, use 4.5 mm needles and add extra rows where indicated. The chart can be used to make the snowflake pattern in either purl stitches, or in a contrasting colour. If you knit the snowflake in purl stitches, try embroidering an outline in a contrasting colour to make the design more visible.

Front

Cast on 33 sts. Beginning with a p row, work 11 rows in st st (or 13 for med).

Next: k8, work row 1 of chart, k8.
Next: p8, work row 2 of chart, p8.

Continue in this pattern, until you finish row 8 of the chart.

Next: k1 skpo, k5, work row 9 of chart, k5, k2tog, k1. (31 sts)
Next: p7, work row 10 of chart, p7.
Next: k1, skpo, k4, work row 11 of chart,

4

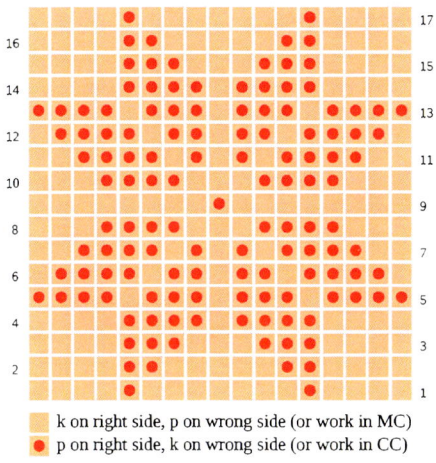

| | | k on right side, p on wrong side (or work in MC) |
| | | p on right side, k on wrong side (or work in CC) |

k4, k2tog, k1. (29 sts) Mark each end of this row.

Next: p6, work row 12 of chart, p6.

Continue, until you finish the chart.

Work 9 rows in st st (or 11 for med).

Next: cast off 7, k15, cast off 7.

Place remaining sts on scrap yarn.

Back

Cast on 33 sts. Beginning with a p row, work 19 rows in st st (or 21 for med).

Next: k1, skpo, k27, k2tog, k1. (31 sts) P 1 row.

Next: k1, skpo, k25, k2tog, k1. (29 sts)
Mark each end of this row.

Work 15 rows in st st (or 17 for med).

Next: cast off 7, k15, cast off 7.

Place remaining sts on scrap yarn.

Collar

Sew together shoulder seams. Place collar sts on dpns (10 sts per needle). Attach yarn to start at left shoulder.

Next: K 1 round, picking up 1 st at each shoulder. (32 sts)

Next: [k4, m1] 3 times, k8, [m1, k4] 3 times. (38 sts)

Work 6 rows in st st.

Cast off all sts loosely.

Sleeves

With right side facing you, pick up 24 sts between markers on front and back.

Next: p24, pick up 1. (25 sts)
Next: k25, pick up 1. (26 sts)
Next: p26, pick up 1. (27 sts)
Next: k27, pick up 1. (28 sts)

Work 15 rows in st st (or 17 for med).

Cast off all sts.

Sew together sleeve and side seams. Secure all yarn ends.

Tip time!

In order for the toy to not look lumpy after you stuff it, first tear off a piece of stuffing about a third larger than the finished piece you are working on. Then roll it in your hands until it is close in shape and size to the toy piece, and gently push it in through the opening in the knitting. Add small extra chunks of stuffing if the piece is not full enough. To smooth out lumps and hollows, insert a darning needle through the side of the toy into the lump and wiggle it around until the lumps are smoothed out and the toy looks nice and even.

REINDEER
WITH A SANTA COAT

REINDEER

Materials

40 g of worsted weight yarn in medium brown (MB), 10 g of worsted weight yarn in dark brown (DB), 5 g of worsted weight yarn in white (W), small amount of yarn for embroidery, two 8 mm (⅜") black buttons or safety eyes, stuffing, pair of 4 mm (US size 6) knitting needles, two 4 mm (US size 6) dpns, tapestry needle

Measurements

23 cm (9") tall

Gauge

22 sts and 32 rows per 10 cm (4")

Legs (make 2)

Begin at sole.

Cast on 10 sts with DB. P 1 row.
Next: k1, [m1, k1] to end. (19 sts)
 P 1 row.
Next: k4, [m1, k3] 5 times. (24 sts)
Starting with a K row, work 5 rows in st st. (this part is reverse st st, i.e. the purl side is on the right side of the piece)
Break off DB, begin next row with MB.
Next: k7, [k2tog] twice, k2, [skpo] twice, k7. (20 sts)
Next: p5, [p2tog tbl] twice, p2, [p2tog] twice, p5. (16 sts)
Next: k7, k2tog, k7. (15 sts)
Work 5 rows in st st.
Next: k2, m1, k11, m1, k2. (17 sts)
Work 11 rows in st st.
Next: k1, [k2tog] 8 times. (9 sts)

Break off yarn. Thread end through remaining stitches, and pull tight to gather. Gather together cast-on stitches at sole, then sew back leg seam, leaving an opening. Stuff and close opening.

Body

The intarsia section is marked with the yarn colour for each set of sts. Begin at neck edge.

Cast on 20 stitches with W.
Starting with a P row, work 5 rows in st st.
Next: [k1, m1, k1] 10 times. (30 sts)
Next: with MB p10, W p10, MB p10.
Next: MB k11, W k8, MB k11.
Next: MB p12, W p6, MB p12.
Work rest of body with MB.
Next: k8, m1, k7, m1, k7, m1, k8. (33 sts)
Work 7 rows in st st.
Next: k15, m1, k3, m1, k15. (35 sts)
Work 3 rows in st st.
Next: k3, m1, k1, m1, k27, m1, k1, m1, k3. (39 sts) P 1 row.
Next: k16, skpo, k3, k2tog, k16. (37 sts)
Work 3 rows in st st.
Next: k15, skpo, k3, k2tog, k15. (35 sts)
Work 3 rows in st st.
Next: K1, [k2tog] to end. (18 sts)
 P 1 row.
Next: [k2tog] to end. (9 sts)

Break off yarn. Thread end through remaining stitches, and pull tight to gather. Sew up back seam to neck edge (leaving neck edge open). Stuff.

Arms (make 2)

Cast on 7 stitches with DB. P 1 row.
Next: k1 [m1, k1] to end. (13 sts)
 P 1 row.
Next: k4, [m1, k3] 3 times. (16 sts)
Starting with a K row, work 5 rows in st st. (this part is reverse st st)
Break off DB, begin next row with MB.
Next: k3, [k2tog] twice, k2, [skpo] twice, k3. (12 sts)
Work 5 rows in st st.
Next: k2, m1, k8, m1, k2. (14 sts)
Work 9 rows in st st.

Next: [k2tog] 7 times. (7 sts)

Break off yarn. Thread end through remaining stitches, and pull tight to gather. Sew back arm seam, leaving an opening. Stuff and close opening.

Head

Begin at back of head.

Cast on 7 sts with MB. P 1 row.

Next: k1, [m1, k1] to end. (13 sts) P 1 row.

Next: k1, [m1, k1] to end. (25 sts)

Work 3 rows in st st.

Next: [k2, m1] 4 times, k9, [m1, k2] 4 times. (33 sts)

Work 11 rows in st st.

Next: [k3, k2tog] 3 times, [k3, skpo] 3 times, k3. (27 sts) P 1 row.

Next: k1, k2tog, k7, k2tog, k3, skpo, k7, skpo, k1. (23 sts) P 1 row.

Next: k1, k2tog, k5, k2tog, k3, skpo, k5, skpo, k1. (19 sts)

Next: k6, k2tog, k3, skpo, k6. (17 sts)

Break off MB, start next row with W.

Work 3 rows in st st.

Next: k1, [k2tog] to end. (9 sts)

Break off yarn. Thread end through remaining stitches, and pull tight to gather. If using safety eyes, attach them to head now. Sew up seam, leaving an opening. Stuff and close opening. Make sure to put extra stuffing in the nose and cheeks to make them stick out.

Ears (make 2)

Cast on 4 sts with MB. K 1 row.

Next: k1, m1, k to end. (5 sts) K 1 row.

Repeat these last 2 rows twice more (7 sts).

Work in garter stitch for 6 rows.

Next: Cast off.

Break off yarn. Fold ear in half along cast-off edge – this edge will be attached to head.

Antlers (make 2)

Using dpns, cast on 4 sts with DB.

Work 5 rows as I-cord, then cast off, leaving a long end for sewing.

Finishing

Sew button eyes in place (or embroider eyes with black yarn if the toy is for a very young child). With length of yarn, embroider nose and mouth. Sew ears in place on head, with curved sides facing outwards. Sew cast-off end of antlers to head, and secure other yarn ends. Sew head securely to open neck edge of body. Thread a length of yarn through left arm about 1cm from top, thread yarn through body at shoulder position, then thread yarn through right arm. Thread yarn through body again, and then the left arm and pull tight. Repeat so yarn passes through each arm 3-4 times. Pull yarn tight so arms are secure, then fasten off yarn. Attach legs at lower edge of body in the same way as the arms.

SANTA COAT

Materials

25 g of worsted weight yarn in red (R), 10 g of worsted weight yarn in white (W), pair of 4 mm (US size 6) knitting needles, 30 cm (12") of ribbon, small buttons (optional), tapestry needle, stitch holder.

Measurements

9 cm (3½") long

Gauge

22 sts and 32 rows per 10 cm (4")

Back

Cast on 30 sts with W.

K 3 rows in garter st.

Break off W, and start next row with R.

Beginning with a K row, work 12 rows in st st.

Next: [k2, k2tog, k1] 6 times. (24 sts)

Work 5 rows in st st. Mark each end of last row.

Next: k1, skpo, k to last 3 sts, k2tog, k1.

P 1 row.

Repeat last 2 rows. (20 sts)

Work 8 rows in st st.

Next: k4, cast off 12, k4.

Next: p4 – these are for left front, place other 4 sts on holder for right front.

Left Front

Next: k1, m1, k to end. P 1 row.

Repeat these 2 rows 3 more times. (8 sts)

Next: k1, m1, k to last st, m1, k1. P 1 row.

Repeat these last 2 rows. (12 sts) Mark beginning of last row.

Work 4 rows in st st.

Next: [k2, m1, k1] 4 times. (16 sts)

Work 12 rows in st st.

Break off R, start next row with W.

P 4 rows in garter st.

Next: cast off all sts.

Right Front

Place 4 sts on needle, with wrong side ready to knit.

Attach R yarn. P 1 row.

Next: k to last st, m1, k1. P 1 row.

Repeat these 2 rows 3 more times. (8 sts)

Next: k1, m1, k to last st, m1, k1. P 1 row.

Repeat these last 2 rows. (12 sts) Mark end of last row.

Work 4 rows in st st.

Next: [k1, m1, k2] 4 times. (16 sts)

Work 12 rows in st st.

Break off R, start next row with W.

P 4 rows in garter st.

Next: cast off all sts.

Secure all yarn ends before making collar.

Collar

With W yarn and right side facing, pick up 19 sts up front edge of right front, 12 sts across back, then 19 sts down front edge of left front. (50 sts)

K 1 row.

Next: k13, m1, [k8, m1] 3 times, k13. (54 sts) K 1 row.

Next: k17, m1, [k4, m1] 5 times, k17. (60 sts)

Next: Cast off 13, k to end. (47 sts)

Next: Cast off 14, k to last 2 sts, k2tog. (32 sts)

Next: p2tog, k28, k2tog. (30 sts)

Next: p2tog, k26, k2tog. (28 sts)

Next: p2tog, cast off all sts.

Sleeves

With R yarn and right side facing, pick up 20 sts between markers on front and back.

Work 8 rows in st st.

Break off R, start next row with W.

P 4 rows in garter st.

Cast off all sts.

Sew together sleeve and side seams. Secure yarn ends. If desired, make button loops on right front, and sew buttons to left front. Tie ribbon around coat waist.

• •

Tip time!

The type of yarn you use for the toy makes a big difference in the final appearance. For a smooth looking toy that is washable and chewable (good for babies) use soft cotton yarns – organic un-dyed cotton is easy to find and is excellent for this purpose. 100% wool is good for a toy that you want to last for a long time, plus it is usually available in a large variety of colours. If you want a fuzzy toy, look for a yarn with some alpaca – the really fuzzy yarns are usually labelled as bulky weight, but knit up just fine on 4 mm (US size 6) needles, and often have enough yardage to make two toys. For rustic and well-textured toys, try hand-spun yarns.

BABY PENGUIN
WITH A HAT AND A SCARF

Penguin

Materials

20 g of worsted weight yarn in grey (G), 10 g of worsted weight yarn in black (B), 10 g of worsted weight yarn in yellow (Y), 5 g of worsted weight yarn in white (W), two 8 mm black buttons or safety eyes, stuffing, pair of 4 mm (US size 6) knitting needles, tapestry needle

Measurements

15 cm (6") tall

Gauge

22 sts and 32 rows per 10 cm (4")

Feet (make 2)

Cast on 10 sts with Y. P 1 row.
Next: k1, [m1, k1] to end. (19 sts)
P 1 row.
Next: k2, m1, k6, m1, k3, m1, k6, m1, k2. (23 sts)
Work 3 rows in st st.
Next: k6, [skpo] twice, k3, [k2tog] twice, k6.
Next: p4, [p2tog] twice, p3, [p2tog tbl] twice, p4.
Next: k6, s1, k2tog, psso, k6. (13 sts)
P 1 row.
Next: k1, [k2tog] across. (7 sts)

Break off yarn. Thread end through remaining stitches, and pull tight to gather. Gather together cast-on sts, then sew back seam, leaving an opening. Stuff and then close opening. Use an extra length of yarn to make stitches to define the toes.

Body

Begin at neck edge.

Cast on 16 stitches with G. P 1 row.
Next: k1, [m1, k1] to end. (31 sts)
Work 3 rows in st st.
Next: k8, m1, k15, m1, k8. (33 sts)
Work 7 rows in st st.
Next: k15, m1, k3, m1, k15. (35 sts)

Work 3 rows in st st.
Next: k3, m1, k1, m1, k27, m1, k1, m1, k3. (39 st) P 1 row.
Next: k16, skpo, k3, k2tog, k16. (37 sts)
Work 3 rows in st st.
Next: k15, skpo, k3, k2tog, k15. (35 sts)
Work 3 rows in st st.
Next: k1, [k2tog] to end. (18 sts) P 1 row.
Next: [k2tog] to end. (9 sts)

Break off yarn. Thread end through remaining stitches and pull tight to gather. Sew up back seam to neck edge (leaving neck edge open). Stuff.

Right wing

Cast on 5 stitches with G. P 1 row.
Next: k1, [m1, k1] to end. P 1 row. (9 sts)
Next: k1, [p1, k1] across. P 1 row.
Next: skpo, k1, [p1, k1] across. P 1 row.
Next: skpo, [p1, k1] across. P 1 row.
Repeat these last 4 rows 3 times. (3 sts)

Break off yarn. Thread end through remaining stitches, pull tight and secure.

Left wing

Cast on 5 stitches with G. P 1 row.
Next: k1, [m1, k1] to end. P 1 row. (9 sts)
Next: k1, [p1, k1] across. P 1 row.
Next: k1, [p1, k1] to last 2 sts, k2tog.
P 1 row.
Next: [k1, p1] to last 2 sts, k2tog.
P 1 row.
Repeat these last 4 rows 3 times. (3 sts)

Break off yarn. Thread end through remaining stitches, pull tight and secure.

Head

Begin at back of head. The intarsia section is marked with the yarn colour for each set of sts.

Cast on 7 sts with B. P 1 row.
Next: k1, [m1, k1] to end. (13 sts)
P 1 row.
Next: k1, [m1, k1] to end. (25 sts)
Work 3 rows in st st.
Next: [k2, m1] 4 times, k9, [m1, k2] 4 times. (33 sts)

Work 7 rows in st st.

Next: W k13, B k7, W k13.

Next: W p13, B p7, W p13.

Repeat these last 2 rows.

Next: W k3, W [k1, k2tog] 3 times, W k1, B k7, W k1, W [skpo, k1] 3 times, W k3. (27 sts)

Next: W p10, B p7, W p10.

Next: W k10, B k7, W k10.

Break off W and B yarns, start next row with Y. P 1 row.

Next: k1, [k2tog] 6 times, k1, [skpo] 6 times, k1. (15 sts) P 1 row.

Next: k3, k2tog, k5, skpo, k3. (13 sts) P 1 row.

Next: k2, k2tog, k5, skpo, k2. (11 sts) P 1 row.

Next: k1, [k2tog] 5 times. (6 sts)

Break off yarn. Thread end through remaining stitches, pull tight to gather. Secure yarn ends from intarsia section. Attach safety eyes. Sew up seam, leaving an opening. Stuff head, making sure to add extra to beak and cheeks, and close opening.

Tail

Cast on 11 sts with G. P 1 row.

Next: k1, [p1, k1] across. P 1 row.

Next: skpo, k1, [p1, k1] 3 times, k2tog. (9 sts) P 1 row.

Next: skpo, [p1, k1] 2 times, p1, k2tog. (7 sts)

Cast off.

Finishing

Sew button eyes in place. Sew head securely to open neck edge of body. Sew top edge of wings at shoulder position on the body. Sew feet securely to body. Sew tail to penguin's bum.

HAT & SCARF

Materials

20 g of worsted weight yarn, set of four 4.5 mm (US size 7) dpns, pair of 4 mm (US size 6) knitting needles, tapestry needle.

Measurements

Hat 10 cm (4") tall; scarf 30 cm (11") long

Gauge

22 sts and 32 rows per 10 cm (4")

Hat

Cast on 32 sts to one dpn. Place 12 sts on first needle, and 10 each on other 2 needles.

Work 3 rounds in k1, p1 rib.

Work 6 rounds in st st.

Next: [k6, k2tog] 4 times. (28 sts)

Work 2 rounds.

Next: [k2, k2tog, k3] 4 times. (24 sts)

Work 2 rounds.

Next: [k4, k2tog] 4 times. (20 sts)

Work 3 rounds.

Next: [k1, k2tog, k2] 4 times. (16 sts)

Work 3 rounds.

Next: [k2, k2tog] 4 times. (12 sts)

Work 3 rounds.

Next: [k2tog, k1] 4 times. (8 sts)

Work 3 rounds.

Break off yarn, thread end through remaining sts, and pull tight to gather. Secure yarn ends. Add tassel, pom-pom, or bell to hat peak.

Scarf

Cast on 63 sts with straight needles.

Next: p3, [k3, p3] across.

Next: k3, [p3, k3] across.

Repeat last 2 rows.

Cast off in pattern. Secure yarn ends, then add fringe to scarf ends.

BIG MAMA BUNNY
WITH AN APRON

Mama Bunny

Materials

100 g of chunky/bulky weight yarn in main colour (MC), 50 g of chunky/ bulky weight yarn in contrasting colour (CC), small amount of yarn for embroidering face, two 12 mm black buttons or safety eyes, stuffing, pair of 5 or 5.5 mm (US size 8 or 9) knitting needles, tapestry needle

Measurements

36 cm (14") tall (without the ears)

Gauge

18 sts and 24 rows per 10 cm (4")

If you use chunky yarn for the bunny, you will want to use 5 mm (US size 8) needles to knit it. If you use bulky yarn, you will want to use 5.5 mm (US size 9) needles.

Legs (make 2)

Cast on 15 sts with CC. P 1 row.
Next: k1, [m1, k1] to end. (29 sts) P 1 row.
Next: k2, [m1, k5] 5 times, m1, k2. (35 sts)
Work 4 rows in st st.
Break off CC, start next row with MC.
Work 3 rows in st st.
Next: k11, [k2tog] 3 times, k1, [skpo] 3 times, k11. (29 sts) P 1 row.
Next: k8, cast off 13 sts, k8. (16 sts)
Next: p8, fold foot to bring next 8 sts to needle point, p8.
Work 4 rows in st st across all 16 sts.
Next: k2, m1, k10, m1, k2. (18 sts)
Work 11 rows in st st.
Next: [k2tog] across. (9 sts)
Break off yarn. Thread end through remaining stitches and pull tight to gather. Sew top of foot together. Sew sole and back leg seam, leaving an opening. Stuff and close opening.

Body

Begin at neck edge.

Cast on 17 stitches with MC. P 1 row.
Next: k1, [m1,k1] to end. (33 sts)
Work 5 rows in st st.
Next: [k8, m1] twice, k1, [m1, k8] twice. (37 sts)
Work 7 rows in st st.
Next: k17, m1, k3, m1, k17. (39 sts)
Work 5 rows in st st.
Next: k4, m1, k1, m1, k29, m1, k1, m1, k4. (43 sts) P 1 row.
Next: k18, skpo, k3, k2tog, k18. (41 sts)
Work 3 rows in st st.
Next: k17, skpo, k3, k2tog, k17. (39 sts)
Work 3 rows in st st.
Next: K1, [k2tog] 17 times. (20 sts) P 1 row.
Next: [k2tog] to end. (10 sts)
Break off yarn. Thread end through remaining stitches, and pull tight to gather. Sew up back seam to neck edge (leaving neck edge open). Stuff.

Right arm

Begin at paw tip.

Cast on 7 stitches with CC. P 1 row.
Next: k1, [m1, k1] to end. (13 sts) P 1 row.
Next: k1, [k1, m1, k2] 4 times. (17 sts)
Work 3 rows in st st.
Break off CC, start next row with MC.
Work 2 rows in st st.
Next: k1, [skpo] twice, k1, [k2tog] twice, k7. (13 sts)
Work 5 rows in st st.
Next: k7, [m1, k3] twice. (15 sts)
Work 11 rows in st st.
Next: k1, [k2tog] 7 times. (8 sts)
Break off yarn. Thread end through remaining stitches, and pull tight to gather. Sew up seam, leaving an opening. Stuff and close opening.

Left arm

Begin at paw tip.

Cast on 7 stitches with CC. P 1 row.

Next: k1, [m1, k1] to end. (13 sts) P 1 row.

Next: k1, [k1, m1, k2] 4 times. (17 sts) Work 3 rows in st st.

Break off CC, start next row with MC. Work 2 rows in st st.

Next: k7, [skpo] twice, k1, [k2tog] twice, k1. (13 sts)

Work 5 rows in st st.

Next: [k3, m1] twice, k7. (15 sts) Work 11 rows in st st.

Next: k1, [k2tog] 7 times. (8 sts)

Break off yarn. Thread end through remaining stitches, and pull tight to gather. Sew up seam, leaving an opening. Stuff and close opening.

Head

Begin at back of head.

Cast on 8 sts with MC. P 1 row.

Next: k1, [m1, k1] to end. (15 sts) P 1 row.

Next: k1, [m1, k1] to end. (29 sts) Work 3 rows in st st.

Next: [k3, m1] 3 times, k11, [m1, k3] 3 times. (35 sts)

Work 13 rows in st st.

Next: k8, [k2tog] twice, k11, [skpo] twice, k8. (31 sts) P 1 row.

Next: k1, [k2tog] 6 times, k5, [skpo] 6 times, k1. (19 sts)

Work 3 rows in st st.

Next: k1, [k2tog] to end. (10 sts)

Break off yarn. Thread end through remaining stitches, and pull tight to gather. If using safety eyes, attach them to head now. Sew up seam, leaving an opening. Stuff and close opening. Make sure to put extra stuffing in the nose to make it stick out.

Ears

Make 2 in MC and 2 in CC.

Cast on 10 sts.

Beginning with a p row, work 3 rows in st st.

Next: k4, m1, k2, m1, k4. (12 sts) P 1 row.

Next: k6, m1, k6. (13 sts)

Working in st st, knit 11 rows for shorter ears, or 17 rows for long ears (bunny in the photo has long ears).

Next: k1, skpo, k to last 3 sts, k2tog, k1. P 1 row.

Repeat these 2 rows until you have 5 sts.

Next: Cast off.

Sew CC ears fronts to MC ear backs along sides and bottom.

Finishing

Sew button eyes in place (or embroider eyes with black yarn if the toy is for a very young child). With length of yarn, embroider nose and mouth. Sew ears in place on head. Sew head securely to open neck edge of body. Thread a length of yarn through left arm about 1 cm (½") from top, thread yarn through body at shoulder position, then thread yarn through right arm. Thread yarn through body again, and then the left arm and pull tight. Repeat so yarn passes through each arm 3-4 times. Pull yarn tight so arms are secure, then fasten off yarn. Attach legs at lower edge of body in the same way as the arms. Make a 4 cm (1½") pom-pom from CC and sew to bunny's bum.

APRON

Materials

25 g of worsted weight yarn, pair of 4.5 mm (US size 7) knitting needles, tapestry/darning needle, two 4.5 mm (US size 7) dpns or 50 cm (20") of 1 cm (⅜") wide ribbon

Measurements

25 cm (10") wide, 10 cm (4") long

Gauge

22 sts and 32 rows per 10 cm (4")

Cast on 31 sts.
Next: p1, [k1, p1] across.
Next: k1, [p1, k1] across.
Next: p1, [k1, p1] across.
Next: [p1, k1] twice, k23, [k1, p1] twice.
Next: [p1, k1] twice, p23, [k1, p1] twice.
Next: [p1, k1] twice, [k1, m1] to last
  5 sts, k1, [k1, p1] twice. (53 sts)
Next: [p1, k1] twice, p45, [k1, p1] twice.
Next: [p1, k1] twice, k45, [k1, p1] twice.
Repeat these 2 rows for a total of 18 rows.
Next: p1, [k1, p1] across.
Repeat this row 3 more times.

Cast off in pattern.

Pocket

Cast on 9 sts.
Beginning with a p row, work 5 rows in
  st st.
Next 2 rows: k1, [p1, k1] across.
Cast off in pattern.

Finishing

Sew pocket to apron front. Make apron
ties by knitting I-cord – two 20 cm (7")
ties – or sewing a ribbon to the waistband.

Baby Bunny

Materials

50 g of DK weight yarn, small amount
of yarn for embroidery, two 8 mm
black buttons or safety eyes, stuffing,
pair of 3.25 mm (US size 3) knitting
needles, darning needle.

Measurements

15 cm (6") tall (excluding ears)

Gauge

26 sts and 34 rows per 10 cm (4")

Legs (make 2)

Cast on 11 sts. P 1 row.
Next: k1, [m1, k1] to end. (21 sts)
  P 1 row.
Next: k3, [m1, k3] 6 times. (27 sts)
Work 5 rows in st st.
Next: k11, k2tog, k1, skpo, k11. (25 sts)
  P 1 row.
Next: k7, cast off 11 sts, k7. (14 sts)
Next: p7, fold foot to bring next 7 sts to
  needle point, p7.
Work 2 rows in st st across all 14 sts.
Next: k2, m1, k10, m1, k2. (16 sts)
Work 9 rows in st st.

Next: [k2tog] 8 times.
Break off yarn. Thread end through remaining stitches and pull tight to gather.
Sew top of foot together. Sew sole and
back leg seam, leaving an opening. Stuff
and close opening.

Body

Begin at neck edge.

Cast on 16 stitches. P 1 row.
Next: k1, [m1, k1] to end. (31 sts)
Work 3 rows in st st.
Next: k8, m1, k15, m1, k8. (33 sts)
Work 3 rows in st st.
Next: k15, m1, k3, m1, k15. (35 sts)
Work 3 rows in st st.
Next: k3, m1, k1, m1, k27, m1, k1, m1,
  k3. (39 st) P 1 row.
Next: k16, skpo, k3, k2tog, k16. (37 sts)
Work 3 rows in st st.
Next: k15, skpo, k3, k2tog, k15. (35 sts)
Work 3 rows in st st.
Next: K1, [k2tog] to end. (18 sts)
  P 1 row.
Next: [k2tog] to end. (9 sts)

Break off yarn. Thread end through remaining stitches and pull tight to gather.
Sew up back seam to neck edge (leaving
neck edge open). Stuff.

BABY BUNNY
WITH A NAPPY AND A BLANKET

Right arm

Begin at paw.

Cast on 6 stitches. P 1 row.

Next: k1, [m1, k1] to end. (11 sts)
  P 1 row.

Next: [k2, m1] twice, k3, [m1, k2] twice.
  (15 sts)

Work 3 rows in st st.

Next: k1, [skpo] twice, [k2tog] twice, k6.
  (11 sts)

Work 3 rows in st st.

Next: k9, m1, k2. (12 sts)

Work 9 rows in st st.

Next: [k2tog] 6 times. (6 sts)

Break off yarn. Thread end through remaining stitches and pull tight to gather.
Sew up seam, leaving an opening. Stuff
and close opening.

Left arm

Begin at paw.

Cast on 6 stitches. P 1 row.

Next: k1, [m1, k1] to end. (11 sts)
  P 1 row.

Next: [k2, m1] twice, k3, [m1, k2] twice.
  (15 sts)

Work 3 rows in st st.

Next: k6, [skpo] twice, [k2tog] twice, k1.
  (11 sts)

Work 3 rows in st st.

Next: k2, m1, k9. (12 sts)

Work 9 rows in st st.

Next: [k2tog] 6 times. (6 sts)

Break off yarn. Thread end through remaining stitches and pull tight to gather.
Sew up seam, leaving an opening. Stuff
and close opening.

Head

Begin at back of head.

Cast on 7 sts. P 1 row.

Next: k1, [m1, k1] to end. (13 sts)
  P 1 row.

Next: k1, [m1, k1] to end. (25 sts)

Work 3 rows in st st.

Next: [k2, m1] 4 times, k9, [m1, k2] 4
  times. (33 sts)

Work 11 rows in st st.

Next: k8, [k2tog] twice, k9, [skpo] twice,
  k8. (29 sts) P 1 row.

Next: k1, [k2tog] 6 times, k3, [skpo] 6
  times, k1. (17 sts)

Work 3 rows in st st.

Next: k1, [k2tog] to end. (9 sts)

Break off yarn. Thread end through remaining stitches and pull tight to gather.
Attach safety eyes if you're using them.
Sew up seam, leaving an opening. Stuff
and close opening.

Ears (make 2)

Cast on 10 sts.

Knit in garter stitch until ear is 4 cm
  (1½") long.

Next: k1, skpo, k to end. K 1 row.

Repeat last two rows. (8 sts)

Next: k1, skpo, k2, k2tog, k1. (6 sts)
  K 1 row.

Next: k1, skpo, k2tog, k1. (4 sts) K 1 row.

Next: k1, skpo, k1. (3 sts)

Break off yarn. Thread end through remaining stitches, pull tight and secure
yarn end.

Finishing

If using button eyes, sew them in place
(or embroider eyes with black yarn if the
toy is for a very young child). Embroider
nose and mouth. Fold cast-on edge of ears
in half, and sew ears in place on head.
Sew head securely to open neck edge of
body. With darning needle, thread a
length of yarn through left arm about
0.5 cm (¼") from top, thread the yarn
through body at shoulder position, then
thread yarn through right arm. Thread
yarn through right arm and body again,
and then the left arm and pull tight. Repeat so yarn passes through each arm 3-4
times. Pull yarn tight so arms are secure,
then fasten off yarn. Attach legs at lower
edge of body in the same way as the
arms. If you like, make a 3 cm (1") dia-
meter pom-pom for a tail and sew securely to the bunny's bum.

NAPPY

Materials

10 g of fingering/sport/baby weight yarn, pair of 3.25 mm (US size 3) needles, two small safety pins (optional), darning needle

Measurements

17cm (6½") around

Gauge

28 sts and 36 rows per 10 cm (4")

Cast on 18 sts. K 4 rows.
Next: k2, p14, k2. K 1 row.
Repeat these 2 rows for total of 5 rows.
Next: k2, skpo, k to last 4 sts, k2tog, k2.
Next: k2, p to last 2 sts, k2.
Repeat these 2 rows until 8 sts remain.
Next: k2, m1, k4, m1, k2. (10 sts)
Next: k2, p6, k2.
Next: k2, m1, [k2, m1] 3 times, k2. (14 sts)
Next: k2, p10, k2.
Next: k2, m1, k10, m1, k2. (16 sts)
Next: k2, p12, k2.
Next: k2, m1, [k2, m1] 6 times, k2. (23 sts)
Next: k2, p to last 2 sts, k2.
Next: k2, m1, k to last 4 sts, m1, k2.
Repeat these last 2 rows until you have 31 sts.

K 3 rows. Cast off.
Secure yarn ends. Fasten back corners to front with small safety pins, or sew back corners in place.

BLANKET

Materials

25 g of fingering/sport/baby weight yarn, pair of 3.25 mm (US size 3) needles, darning needle

Measurements

19 cm (7.5") wide

Gauge

28 sts and 36 rows per 10 cm (4")

Cast on 53 sts. K 1 row.
Work in stitch pattern until blanket is as long as you want, making sure to end with row 4.
Work row 1, then cast off all sts.

Stitch pattern:

Row 1: p1, [k3, p1] across.
Row 2: k across.
Row 3: k1, [k1, p1, k2] across.
Row 4: k across.

Knit the blanket in one colour, or make stripes which are 4 rows wide. If you make a striped blanket, you may want to crochet around the edges of the finished blanket to make the edges look tidier.

Tip time!

If you do not want to use buttons or safety eyes, you can embroider the eyes by making a short vertical stitch with some black yarn, and then going over it 2-4 times to make it thicker. Alternatively, cut a small circle from black felt and carefully stitch it in place with black thread and a hand-sewing needle. You can add small dots to the eyes with white yarn or white acrylic paint in order to make them look less flat.

If you are good at embroidery and want more elaborate eyes on your toys, you can stitch coloured irises and black pupils onto white oval-shaped pieces of felt.

Squirrel
with Overalls

Squirrel

Materials

50 g of worsted weight yarn, 15 g of polyester eyelash yarn (with long fringe), small amount of yarn for embroidery, two 8 mm black buttons or safety eyes, stuffing, pair of 4 mm (US size 6) knitting needles, tapestry needle

Measurements

20 cm (8") tall

Gauge

22 sts and 32 rows to 10 cm (4")

Legs (make 2)

Begin at sole.

Cast on 10 sts. P 1 row.
Next: k1, [m1, k1] to end. (19 sts)
  P 1 row.
Next: k4, [m1, k3] 5 times. (24 sts)
Work 3 rows in st st.
Next: k8, [skpo] twice, [k2tog] twice, k8. (20 sts)
Next: p6, [p2tog] twice, [p2tog tbl] twice, p6. (16 sts)
Next: k7, k2tog, k7. (15 sts)
Work 3 rows in st st.
Next: k2, m1, k11, m1, k2. (17 sts)
Work 11 rows in st st.
Next: k1, [k2tog] 8 times. (9 sts)

Break off yarn. Thread end through remaining stitches and pull tight to gather. Sew up sole and back leg seam, leaving an opening. Stuff and close opening.

Body

Begin at neck edge.

Cast on 16 stitches. P 1 row.
Next: k1, [m1, k1] to end. (31 sts)
Work 3 rows in st st.
Next: k8, m1, k15, m1, k8. (33 sts)
Work 7 rows in st st.
Next: k15, m1, k3, m1, k15. (35 sts)
Work 3 rows in st st.

Next: k3, m1, k1, m1, k27, m1, k1, m1, k3. (39 sts) P 1 row.
Next: k16, skpo, k3, k2tog, k16. (37 sts)
Work 3 rows in st st.
Next: k15, skpo, k3, k2tog, k15. (35 sts)
Work 3 rows in st st.
Next: k1, [k2tog] to end. (18 sts) P 1 row.
Next: [k2tog] to end. (9 sts)

Break off yarn. Thread end through remaining stitches and pull tight to gather. Sew up back seam to neck edge (leaving neck edge open). Stuff body.

Right arm

Begin at paw tip.

Cast on 6 stitches. P 1 row.
Next: k1, [m1, k1] to end. (11 sts)
  P 1 row.
Next: [k2, m1] twice, k3, [m1, k2] twice. (15 sts)
Work 3 rows in st st.
Next: k1, [skpo] twice, [k2tog] twice, k6. (11 sts)
Work 5 rows in st st.
Next: k5, [m1, k3] twice. (13 sts)
Work 9 rows in st st.
Next: k1, [k2tog] 6 times. (7 sts)

Break off yarn. Thread end through remaining stitches and pull tight to gather. Sew up seam, leaving an opening. Stuff and close opening.

Left arm

Begin at paw tip.

Cast on 6 stitches. P 1 row.
Next: k1, [m1, k1] to end. (11 sts)
  P 1 row.
Next: [k2, m1] twice, k3, [m1, k2] twice. (15 sts)
Work 3 rows in st st.
Next: k6, [skpo] twice, [k2tog] twice, k1. (11 sts)
Work 5 rows in st st.
Next: k3, m1, k3, m1, k5. (13 sts)
Work 9 rows in st st.
Next: k1, [k2tog] 6 times. (7 sts)

Break off yarn. Thread end through remaining stitches and pull tight to gather. Sew up seam, leaving an opening. Stuff and close opening.

Head

Cast on 7 sts. P 1 row.

Next: k1, [m1, k1] to end. (13 sts)
  P 1 row.

Next: k1, [m1, k1] to end. (25 sts)

Work 3 rows in st st.

Next: [k2, m1] 4 times, k9, [m1, k2]
  4 times. (33 sts)

Work 11 rows in st st.

Next: k8, [k2tog] twice, k9, [skpo] twice,
  k8. (29 sts) P 1 row.

Next: k1, [k2tog] 6 times, k3, [skpo]
  6 times, k1. (17 sts)

Work 3 rows in st st.

Next: k1, [k2tog] to end. (9 sts)

Break off yarn. Thread end through re-maining stitches and pull tight to gather. Attach safety eyes to head now. Sew up seam, leaving an opening. Stuff and close opening. Make sure to put a bit of extra stuffing in the nose and cheeks to make them stick out.

Ears (make 2)

Cast on 7 sts. K 1 row.

Next: k1, skpo, k to end.

Repeat last 2 rows until 5 sts remain.

Next: k1, skpo, k2 tog. K 1 row.

Break off yarn. Thread end through re-maining stitches, pull tight and secure.

Tail

Cast on 13 sts.

Work 3 rows in st st.

Next: k1, [m1, k1] to end. (25 sts)

Work in st st until tail is about 12-15 cm
  (5-6") long, ending with a P row.

Next: [k3, k2tog] 5 times. (20 sts)
  P 1 row.

Next: [k2, k2tog] 5 times. (15 sts)
  P 1 row.

Next: [k1, k2tog] 5 times. (10 sts)

Break of yarn, thread end through remain-ing sts, and stitch together edges of tail to

make a tube (with knit side out). You can use a comb to gently fluff out the tail.

Finishing

Sew button eyes in place (or embroider eyes with black yarn if the toy is for a very young child). Embroider nose and mouth. Sew cast-on edge of ears in place on head. Sew head securely to open neck edge of body. Thread a length of yarn through left arm about 1 cm (½") from top, thread yarn through body at shoulder position, then thread yarn though right arm. Thread yarn through body again, and then the left arm and pull tight. Repeat so yarn passes through each arm 3-4 times. Pull yarn tight so arms are secure, then fasten off yarn. Attach legs at lower edge of body in the same way as the arms. Stitch tail securely to the squirrel's bum.

OVERALLS

Materials

25 g of worsted weight yarn, 2 small buttons, pair of 4 mm (US size 6) knitting needles, tapestry needle

Measurements

17 cm (7") around, 10 cm (4") long

Gauge

22 sts and 32 rows to 10 cm (4")

Left Leg

Begin at bottom of leg, end at waist.

*Cast on 24 sts. K 1 row.

Starting with a K row, work 6 rows in
  st st.

Next: k1, m1, k22, m1, k1. (26 sts)
  P 1 row.

Next: k1, m1, k24, m1, k1. (28 sts)
  P 1 row.

Mark each end of this last row.

Next: k1, skpo, k22, k2tog, k1. (26 sts)
  P 1 row.

Next: k1, skpo, k20, k2tog, k1. (24 sts)
  P 1 row.

Next: k1, skpo, k18, k2tog, k1. (22 sts)
Starting with a P row, work 9 rows in st st.**
Next: p16, k6. P 1 row.
Next: p16, k6.
Next: cast off all sts.

Right Leg

Follow pattern for left leg from * to **
Next: k6, p16. P 1 row.
Next: k6, p16.
Next: cast off all sts.

Sew together front seam of legs from waist to markers (leg fronts are st st at waist, backs are garter st)

Bib

With right side facing you, pick up 7 sts on each side of front seam (14 sts).
Next: k2, p10, k2. K 1 row.

Repeat these 2 rows 3 more times. (8 rows total)
Knit 3 rows in garter stitch.
Next: Cast off all sts.

Straps (make 2)

Pick up 4 sts from waist edge, 1 cm (½") from centre back edge.
Work in garter st until strap is 6.5 cm (2½") long.
Next: k2, yo, k2. (5 sts) K 1 row.
Next: skpo, k1, k2tog. (3 sts)

Break off yarn and thread end through remaining sts. Secure yarn end.

Sew together back seam of legs from waist edge to markers, leaving a gap for the tail. Sew together crotch seam. Sew buttons on bib corners. Cross straps in back and button ends to bib.

• •

KOALA

Materials

50 g of worsted weight yarn in grey (G), 10 g of worsted weight yarn in white (W), small amount of black yarn for embroidery, two 8 mm black buttons or safety eyes, stuffing, pair of 4 mm (US size 6) knitting needle, tapestry needle

Measurements

17 cm (7") tall

Gauge

22 sts and 32 rows per 10 cm (4")

Legs (make 2)

Start at sole.

Cast on 10 sts with G. P 1 row.
Next: k1, [m1, k1] to end. (19 sts) P 1 row.

Next: k4, [m1, k3] 5 times. (24 sts)
Work 3 rows in st st.
Next: k8, [skpo] twice, [k2tog] twice, k8. (20 sts)
Next: p6, [p2tog] twice, [p2tog tbl] twice, p6. (16 sts)
Next: k7, k2tog, k7. (15 sts)
Work 3 rows in st st.
Next: k2, m1, k11, m1, k2. (17 sts)
Work 9 rows in st st.
Next: k1, [k2tog] 8 times. (9 sts)

Break off yarn. Thread end through remaining stitches and pull tight to gather. Sew up sole and back leg seam, leaving an opening. Stuff and close opening.

Body Back

Start at neck edge.

Cast on 9 sts with G. P 1 row.
Next: k1, [m1, k1] to end. (17 sts)
Work 5 rows in st st.
Next: k2, m1, k13, m1, k2. (19 sts)
Work 9 rows in st st.

SURFER KOALA
WITH SWIMMING TRUNKS

Next: k6, m1, k1, m1, k5, m1, k1, m1, k6. (23 sts)
Work 9 rows in st st.
Next: k1, [k2tog] to end. (12 sts) P 1 row.
Next: k2, [k2tog] 4 times, k2. (8 sts)
Cast off all sts.

Body Front

Start at neck edge.

Cast on 8 sts with W. P 1 row.
Next: k1, [m1, k1] to end. (15 sts)
Work 3 rows in st st.
Next: k7, m1, k1, m1, k7. (17 sts)
Work 7 rows in st st.
Next: k7, m1, k3, m1, k7. (19 sts)
Work 5 rows in st st.
Next: k6, skpo, k3, k2tog, k6. (17 sts)
Work 3 rows in st st.
Next: k5, skpo, k3, k2tog, k5. (15 sts)
Work 3 rows in st st.
Next: k1, [k2tog] to end. (8 sts)
Next: Cast off all sts.

Sew back to front along side and bottom seams, leaving cast on (neck) edge open. Stuff body.

Right arm

Begin at paw tip.

Cast on 6 stitches with G. P 1 row.
Next: k1, [m1, k1] to end. (11 sts)
  P 1 row.
Next: [k2, m1] twice, k3, [m1, k2] twice. (15 sts)
Work 3 rows in st st.
Next: k1, [skpo] twice, [k2tog] twice, k6. (11 sts)
Work 5 rows in st st.
Next: k5, [m1, k3] twice. (13 sts)
Work 9 rows in st st.
Next: k1, [k2tog] 6 times. (7 sts)

Break off yarn. Thread end through remaining stitches and pull tight to gather. Sew up seam, leaving an opening. Stuff and close opening.

Left arm

Begin at paw tip.

Cast on 6 stitches with G. P 1 row.
Next: k1, [m1, k1] to end. (11 sts)
  P 1 row.
Next: [k2, m1] twice, k3, [m1, k2] twice. (15 sts)
Work 3 rows in st st.
Next: k6, [skpo] twice, [k2tog] twice, k1. (11 sts)
Work 5 rows in st st.
Next: k3, m1, k3, m1, k5. (13 sts)
Work 9 rows in st st.
Next: k1, [k2tog] 6 times. (7 sts)

Break off yarn. Thread end through remaining stitches and pull tight to gather. Sew up seam, leaving an opening. Stuff and close opening.

Head

Begin at back of head.

Cast on 7 sts with G. P 1 row.
Next: k1, [m1, k1] to end. (13 sts)
  P 1 row.
Next: k1, [m1, k1] to end. (25 sts)
Work 3 rows in st st.
Next: [k2, m1] 4 times, k9, [m1, k2] 4 times. (33 sts)
Work 11 rows in st st.
Next: k8, [k2tog] twice, k9, [skpo] twice, k8. (29 sts) P 1 row.
Next: k1, [k2tog] 6 times, k3, [skpo] 6 times, k1. (17 sts)
Work 3 rows in st st.
Next: k1, [k2tog] to end. (9 sts)

Break off yarn. Thread end through remaining stitches and pull tight to gather. Attach safety eyes to head now. Sew up seam, leaving an opening. Stuff and close opening. Make sure to put a bit of extra stuffing in the nose and cheeks to make them stick out.

Ears

Make 2 in G and 2 in W.

Cast on 10 sts. P 1 row
Next: k1, m1, k8, m1, k1. (12 sts)
Work 5 rows in st st.
Next: k1, skpo, k6, k2tog, k1. (10 sts)

P 1 row.

Next: cast off.

Sew white ear fronts to grey ear backs.

Finishing

Sew button eyes in place (or embroider eyes with black yarn if the toy is for a very young child). With black yarn, embroider nose and mouth. Sew cast-on edge of ears in place on head. Sew head securely to open neck edge of body. Thread a length of yarn through left arm about 1 cm (½") from top, thread yarn through body at shoulder position, then thread yarn through right arm. Thread yarn through body again, and then the left arm and pull tight. Repeat so yarn passes through each arm 3-4 times. Pull yarn tight so arms are secure, then fasten off yarn. Attach legs at lower edge of body in the same way as the arms.

SWIMMING TRUNKS

Legs (make 2)

Cast on 26 sts. Work 3 rows in k1, p1 rib. Starting with a k row, work 14 rows in st st.

Materials

15 g of sport weight yarn, pair of 3 mm (US size 2.5) knitting needles, tapestry needle

Measurements

17 cm (7") around, 6 cm (2.5") long

Gauge

26 sts and 34 rows per 10 cm (4")

Next: k1, m1, k to last st, m1, k1. P 1 row.

Repeat last 2 rows twice more (32 sts) Mark each end of last row.

Next: k1, skpo, k24, k2tog, k1. P 1 row.

Repeat these last 2 rows once more. (28 sts)

Work 2 rows in st st.

Next: cast off.

Sew front and back seams from ribbed edge to marks. Sew together crotch seams. Thread extra length of yarn around waistband, and tie in front.

• •

Tip time!

A diagram for how to attach the arms and legs. Follow the directions of the arrows, making the stitch across the top of the arm or leg horizontal, rather than vertical as it seems in the diagram. Do this 3-4 times, snugging up the yarn with each pass through the body so the pieces are firmly attached. Then secure the yarn ends.

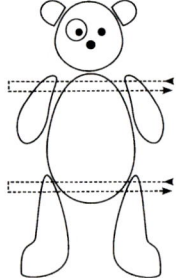

FUZZY FARM

WITH AN OINK-OINK HERE, AND AN OINK-OINK THERE

Fuzzy Farm

Materials

Pig: 15 g of white worsted weight yarn, yarn to embroider face, stuffing, pair of 4 mm (US size 6) needles, two 4 mm double pointed needles (dpns), darning needle.

Sheep: 15 g of white (W) worsted weight yarn, 10 g of gray (G) worsted weight yarn, yarn to embroider face, stuffing, pair of 4 mm (US size 6) needles, two 4mm dpns, darning needle.

Chicken: 15 g of brown worsted weight yarn, yarn to embroider face, stuffing, pair of 4mm (US size 6) needles, darning needle.

Measurements

Pig: 7.5 cm (3") tall, 10 cm (4") long
Sheep: 10 cm (4") tall, 11 cm (4½") long
Chicken: 7.5 cm (3") tall, 7.5 cm (3") long

Gauge

22 sts and 32 rows to 10 cm (4")

You can try knitting these guys from different yarn weights, using appropriate size needles, to get smaller or larger animals.

PIG

Body

Cast on 7 sts. P 1 row.
Next: k1, [m1, k1] to end. (13 sts) P 1 row.
Next: k1, [m1, k1] to end. (25 sts)
Work 3 rows in st st.
Next: [k2, m1, k3] 5 times. (30 sts)
Work 13 rows in st st.
Next: k12, k2tog, k2, skpo, k12. (28 sts) P 1 row.
Next: k11, k2tog, k2, skpo, k11. (26 sts) P 1 row.
Next: skpo, k8, k2tog, k2, skpo, k8, k2tog. (22 sts) P 1 row.
Next: skpo, k6, k2tog, k2, skpo, k6, k2tog. (18 sts) P 1 row.
Next: k1, [k2tog] 4 times, [skpo] 4 times, k1. (10 sts)
Next: P 1 row, then K 3 rows.

Break off yarn, thread end through sts and pull tight. Use yarn ends to sew up tummy seam, stuffing body before closing seam. Embroider eyes and mouth. Make a short braid for the pig's tail.

Ears (make 2)

Cast on 6 sts. K 2 rows.
Next: k3, k2tog, k1. (5 sts) K 1 row.
Next: k2, k2tog, k1. (4 sts) K 1 row.
Next: k1, k2tog, k1. (3 sts) K 1 row.

Break off yarn, thread end through sts and pull tight. Secure yarn end. Sew cast-on edge of ears to head.

Legs (make 4)

Knit as I-cord on 2 dpns.

Cast on 5 sts.
Work 7 rows, or until leg is 4 cm (1½") long.

Break off yarn, thread end through sts and pull tight. Sew legs to underside of body.

SHEEP

Body

Cast on 9 sts with W yarn. P 1 row.
Next: k1, [m1, k1] to end. (17 sts) P 1 row.
Next: k1, [m1, k1] to end. (33 sts)
Work 3 rows in st st.
Next: k3, [m1, k5] 6 times. (39 sts)
Work 11 rows in st st. (If you would like the body longer, add another 2 or 4 rows)
Next: skpo, k35, k2tog. (37 sts) P 1 row.
Next: skpo, k12, k2tog, k5, skpo, k12, k2tog. (33 sts) P 1 row.
Next: [skpo] twice, k7, [k2tog] twice, k3, [skpo] twice, k7, [k2tog] twice. (25 sts)

Break off W yarn, start next row with G yarn – purl stitches face out on body, and knit stitches face out on head.

Next: k9, k2tog, k3, skpo, k9. (23 sts)
  P 1 row.
Next: k8, k2tog, k3, skpo, k8. (21 sts)
  P 1 row.
Next: k7, k2tog, k3, skpo, k7. (19 sts)
Work 3 rows in st st.
Next: k1, [k2tog] 9 times. (10 sts)

Break off yarn, thread end through stitches and pull tight. Sew up tummy seam with knit stitches facing out on face, and purl stitches facing out on body. Stuff body before closing up seam. Embroider eyes, nose and mouth.

Ears

Cast on 4 sts with G yarn.
K 1 row.
Next: k3, m1, k1. (5 sts) K 1 row.
Next: k4, m1, k1. (6 sts) K 1 row.
Next: k5, m1, k1. (7 sts)
Knit 5 rows in garter st. Cast off all sts.

Fold ears in half, and sew cast-off edge of ears to head.

Legs

Knit in G yarn, same as for pig.

CHICKEN

Body

Cast on 25 sts. P 1 row,
Next: k1, m1, k9, k2tog, k1, skpo, k9, m1, k1. P 1 row.

Repeat last 2 rows twice more.
Next: k1, m1, k23, m1, k1. (27 sts)
Work 5 rows in st st.
Next: k12, m1, k3, m1, k12. (29 sts)
  P 1 row.
Next: k13, m1, k3, m1, k13. (31 sts)
  P 1 row.
Next: [skpo] 5 times, k4, m1, k3, m1, k4, [k2tog] 5 times. (23 sts) P 1 row.
Next: [skpo] 3 times, k4, m1, k3, m1, k4, [k2tog] 3 times. (19 sts)
Next: cast off 4 sts, p to end of row. (15 sts)
Next: cast off 4 sts (1 st remaining on needle), k3, m1, k3, m1, k4. (13 sts)
Work 2 rows in st st.
Next: p1, [p2tog] 6 times. (7 sts)

Break off yarn, thread end through stitches and pull tight. Sew up tummy seam with yarn ends, stuffing body before closing up seam. Embroider eyes and beak. Embroider feet if you like.

Wings (make 2)

Cast on 11 sts.
Next: K 3 rows.
Next: k1, skpo, k to end.
Repeat this last row until 3 sts remain.

Break off yarn, thread end through stitches and pull tight. Sew wings to body, using yarn end left from casting on.

• •

Tip time!

Variegated or self-striping yarns are great to use for the toy clothes. Most outfits will only require what you might have lying around left over from knitting a pair of socks.

PIRATE HIPPO
WITH A PARROT

HIPPO

Materials

50 g of grey worsted weight yarn, small amount of pink worsted weight yarn, two 8 mm black buttons or safety eyes, black yarn for embroidery, small piece of white felt, white thread, stuffing, pair of 4 mm (US size 6) knitting needles, stitch holder, tapestry needle, hand-sewing needle

Measurements

20 cm (8") tall

Gauge

22 sts and 32 rows per 10 cm (4")

All the pieces are knit in the grey yarn, except the mouth.

Legs (make 2)

Cast on 10 sts. P 1 row.
Next: k1, [m1, k1] to end. P 1 row. (19 sts)
Next: k2, m1, k6, m1, k3, m1, k6, m1, k2. (23 sts)
Next: P 3 rows.
Next: k2, skpo, k15, k2tog, k2. (21 sts) P 1 row.
Next: k5, [k2tog] twice, k3, [skpo] twice, k5. (17 sts)
Work 7 rows in st st.
Next: k2, k2tog, k9, skpo, k2. (15 sts)
Work 5 rows in st st.
Next: k1, [k2tog] 7 times. (8 sts) P 1 row.
Next: [k2tog] 4 times. (4 sts)
Break off yarn. Thread end through remaining stitches, pull tight and secure. Join sole and back leg seam, leaving an opening. Stuff and close opening.

Body

Begin at neck edge.

Cast on 15 stitches. P 1 row.
Next: k1 [m1, k1] to end. (29 sts)
Work 5 rows in st st.
Next: [k7, m1] twice, k1, [m1, k7] twice.
(33 sts)
Work 5 rows in st st.
Next: k15, m1, k3, m1, k15. (35 sts)
Work 3 rows in st st.
Next: k3, m1, k1, m1, k27, m1, k1, m1, k3. P 1 row. (39 sts)
Next: k16, skpo, k3, k2tog, k16. (37 sts)
Work 3 rows in st st.
Next: k15, skpo, k3, k2tog, k15. (35 sts)
Work 3 rows in st st.
Next: K1, [k2tog] to end. P1 row. (18 sts)
Next: [k2tog] to end. (9 sts)
Break off yarn. Thread end through remaining stitches, pull tight and secure. Sew up back seam to neck edge (leaving neck edge open). Stuff.

Arms (make 2)

Cast on 6 stitches. P 1 row.
Next: k1, [m1, k1] to end. P 1 row.
(11 sts)
Next: [k2, m1] twice, k3, [m1, k2] twice.
(15 sts)
Work 3 rows in st st.
Next: k4, k2tog, k3, skpo, k4. (13 sts)
Work 7 rows in st st
Next: k1, skpo, k7, k2tog, k1. (11 sts)
Work 5 rows in st st.
Next: k1, [k2tog] 5 times. (6 sts)
Break off yarn. Thread end through remaining stitches, pull tight and secure. Sew up seam, leaving an opening. Stuff and close opening.

Head

Begin at back.

Cast on 6 sts. P 1 row.
Next: k1, [m1, k1] to end. (11 sts)
P 1 row.
Next: k1, [m1, k1] to end. (21 sts)
Work 3 rows in st st.
Next: k1, [m1, k4] 5 times. (26 sts)
Work 11 rows in st st.
Next: k9, k2tog, k4, skpo, k9. (24 sts)
P 1 row.
Next: k8, k2tog, k4, skpo, k8 (22 sts)
P 1 row.

Next: k1, m1, k4 - place these first 6 sts on holder, k2, [m1, k1] nine times, k5, m1, k1 - place these last 6 sts on holder.

Break off yarn. Attach yarn to sts still on needle. (21 sts) This next part makes the nose.

Next: P 1 row.

Next: k1, m1, k19, m1, k1. (23 sts) Work 3 rows in st st.

Next: k7, k2tog, k5, skpo, k7. (21 sts) P 1 row.

Next: skpo, k4, k2tog, k5, skpo, k4, k2tog. (17 sts) P 1 row.

Next: skpo, k2, k2tog, k5, skpo, k2, k2tog. (13 sts)

Next: p2tog, [p2tog tbl] twice, k1, [p2tog] twice, p2tog tbl. (7 sts)

Cast off 7 sts.

Place 12 sts from holder onto needle so wrong side is facing you - you're joining the 2 sides together to make the underside of the chin in one piece. Attach yarn.

Next: p5, p2tog, p5. (11 sts) Work 4 rows in st st.

Next: skpo, k7, k2tog. (9 sts) P 1 row

Next: skpo, k5, k2tog. (7 sts)

Next: p2tog, p3, p2tog tbl. (5 sts)

Cast off 5 sts.

Mouth

Knit mouth with pink yarn.

Cast on 7 sts. P 1 row.

Next: k1, m1, k5, m1, k1. (9 sts) P 1 row.

Next: k1, m1, k7, m1, k1. (11 sts) Work 5 rows in st st.

Next: skpo, k7, k2tog. (9 sts) P 1 row.

Next: skpo, k5, k2tog. (7 sts) P 1 row.

Next: k1, m1, k5, m1, k1. (9 sts) Work 5 rows in st st.

Next: skpo, k5, k2tog. (7 sts)

Next: p2tog, p3, p2tog tbl. (5 sts)

Cast off 5 sts.

Ears (make 2)

Cast on 5 sts.

Beginning with a P row, work 5 rows in st st.

Next: skpo, k1, k2tog. (3 sts)

Break off yarn, thread end through 3 sts, pull tight and secure end.

Finishing

Head: If you're using safety eyes, attach them to the head now. The next step is to sew the mouth to the head. The mouth should look like a pear – the wider end matches to the top of the mouth, the narrower end matches to the bottom of the mouth. Carefully sew the mouth to the head all around the edges. It helps to start at the forward edges (i.e. the lips) and work towards the corners of the mouth along both sides. Secure all the yarn ends, then stuff the head – the lower jaw doesn't need any stuffing. Sew up the seam along the bottom. Sew on the button eyes. Fold ears in half lengthwise, then sew onto the head. Embroider nose holes and a smile. Cut two 1 cm (⅜") squares from the white felt, and sew them to the top jaw using the hand-sewing needle and thread. If you have some red yarn, make a tongue in duplicate stitch inside the mouth.

Rest of toy: Sew head securely to the open neck edge of the body. Thread a length of yarn through the left arm about 1 cm (¼") from top, thread yarn through the body at shoulder position, then thread yarn though the right arm. Thread back through right arm, body, and then the left arm and pull tight. Repeat so yarn passes through each arm 3-4 times. Pull yarn tight so arms are secure, then fasten off yarn. Attach legs at lower edge of body in the same way as the arms. To make the tail: attach 3 lengths of yarn to bum, braid the yarn, tie a knot once the braid is long enough, and trim the extra yarn.

SHIRT

Materials

15 g of fingering weight yarn in white (W) and contrasting colour (C), pair of 2.75 mm (US size 2) knitting needles

Measurements

18 cm (7") around, 8 cm (3") long

Gauge

28 sts and 36 rows per 10 cm (4")

Front and back

Cast on 30 sts with C yarn.

Next: [k1, p1] across for 2 rows.

For rest of shirt, stripe in 2 rows W, 2 rows C.

Starting with a p row, work in st st for 13 rows. Mark each end of last row.

Next: k1, skpo, k to last 3 sts, k2tog, k1. (28 sts) P 1 row.

Repeat last 2 rows. (26 sts)

Work in st st for 12 rows.

Next: k6, cast off 14, k6. (or cast off all sts if you don't want to graft shoulder seams)

Sleeves

Same for right and left. Graft or sew together shoulder seams. With right side facing you, with W yarn pick up 24 sts between markers on front and back.

For rest of sleeve, stripe in 2 rows W, 2 rows C.

Starting with a purl row, work 11 rows in st st.

Next: [k1, p1] across.

Next: cast off in rib.

Sew together side and sleeve seams.

PARROT

Materials

Small amount of red worsted weight yarn, scraps of yellow, blue and green yarn, small amount of white felt, 2 small black beads or black embroidery floss, pair of 4 mm (US size 6) knitting needles, small crochet hook

Measurements

6.5 cm (2½") long

Gauge

22 sts and 32 rows per 10 cm (4")

Cast on 5 sts. P 1 row.

Next: k1, m1, k3, m1, k1. (7 sts)

Work 3 rows in st st.

Next: k1, m1, k1, m1, k3, m1, k1, m1, k1. (11 sts)

Work 5 rows in st st.

Next: skpo, k7, k2tog. (9 sts) P 1 row.

Next: skpo, k5, k2tog. (7 sts) P 1 row.

Next: skpo, k3, k2tog. (5 sts) P 1 row.

Next: skpo, k1, k2tog. (3 sts)

Break off yarn, thread end through 3 sts remaining, and pull tight. Use yarn end to sew front seam towards cast-on edge (head), adding stuffing before closing seam. Use yellow yarn to embroider beak and feet. Cut two 1 cm (⅜") circles from white felt. Place one on each side of head, then sew on bead eyes or embroider with black floss. Cut green and blue yarn into 7 cm (3") pieces and knot onto body to make wings and tail, then trim to the length you like. To knot: fold in half, pull under a stitch with the crochet hook, then pull the ends through the loop and snug tight.

BATTY BAT
WITH A JACK O'LANTERN

BAT

Materials

50 g worsted weight yarn in main colour (MC), 15 g of worsted weight yarn in contrasting colour (CC), small amount of yarn for embroidery, two 8 mm black buttons or safety eyes, stuffing, set of four 4 mm dpns, pair of 4 mm knitting needles, darning needle, crochet hook, scrap yarn, 2 stitch markers.

Measurements

20 cm (8") tall, 35 cm (14") wingspan

Gauge

22 sts and 32 rows per 10cm (4")

Legs (make 2)

Knit with dpns.

Cast on 9 sts with MC, distribute between needles (3 sts per needle). K 1 round.
Next: [k1, m1] around. (18 sts) K 1 round.
Next: [k3, m1] 6 times. (24 sts) K 3 rounds.
Next: k8, [skpo] twice, [k2tog] twice, k8. (20 sts)
Next: k6, [skpo] twice, [k2tog] twice, k6. (16 sts)
You will want to redistribute sts on needles before continuing.
Next: k7, k2tog, k7. (15 sts) K 2 rounds.
Next: k2, m1, k11, m1, k2. (17 sts) K 3 rounds.
Break off yarn. Place sts on scrap yarn.

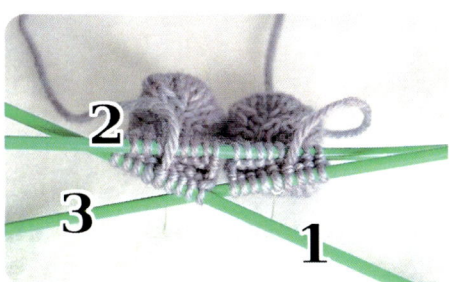

Body

Place leg sts back onto dpns, in order listed below (see figure).

needle 1: 5 sts to right of yarn end of leg one + 4 sts to left of yarn end of leg one (9 sts)
needle 3: 4 sts to right of yarn end of leg two + 5 sts to left of yarn end of leg two (9 sts)
needle 2: 8 sts across the front leg leg one + 8 sts across the front of leg 2 (16 sts)

Altogether you should have 34 sts. Attach MC yarn to start with needle one (this is the centre back of the body)

Next: k16, k2tog, k16. (33 sts)
Next: [k3, m1] twice, k21, [m1, k3] twice. (37 sts) K 1 round.
Next: k17, m1, k3, m1, k17. (39 sts) K 7 rounds.
Next: [k2, k2tog] twice, k23, [skpo, k2] twice. (35 sts) K 3 rounds.
Next: k14, skpo, k3, k2tog, k14. (33 sts) K 4 rounds.
Next: k5, skpo, k6, skpo, k3, k2tog, k6, k2tog, k5. (29 sts) K 3 rounds.
Next: k2, [skpo] 6 times, k1, [k2tog] 6 times, k2. (17 sts) K 1 round.
Cast off all sts.

Gather together cast on sts on feet bottoms, and thread yarn ends to inside of body. Turn body inside out, sew up hole between legs, and secure all yarn ends. Turn body right side out, and stuff through neck opening (leave neck open for sewing to head).

Head

Knit head on pair of 4 mm needles.

Cast on 7 sts with MC. P 1 row.
Next: k1, [m1, k1] to end. (13 sts) P 1 row.
Next: k1, [m1, k1] to end. (25 sts) Work 3 rows in st st.
Next: [k2, m1] 4 times, k9, [m1, k2] 4 times. (33 sts)
Work 11 rows in st st.

Next: k8, [k2tog] twice, k9, [skpo] twice, k8. (29 sts) P 1 row.

Next: k1, [k2tog] 6 times, k3, [skpo] 6 times, k1. (17 sts) P 1 row.

Next: k1, k2tog, k4, m1, k3, m1, k4, skpo, k1. P 1 row.

Repeat last 2 rows.

Next: [skpo] 3 times, k5, [k2tog] 3 times. (11 sts)

Graft together remaining sts, use 3-needle bind off, or cast off and use fake grafting to sew nose end. Attach safety eyes. Gather together cast-on sts, then sew up seam along bottom of head, leaving a small opening. Stuff the head, making sure to put extra stuffing in the nose so it sticks out. Close opening.

Right Wing

Knit wing with pair of 4 mm needles.

Cast on 43 sts with CC.

K 3 rows in garter stitch.

Next: k1, skpo, k9, PM, skpo, k9, PM, skpo, k to end. (40 sts) P 1 row.

Next: k1, skpo, [k to M, skpo] twice, k to end. P 1 row.

Repeat last 2 rows until 13 sts remain.

Break off CC, start next row with MC.

Next: k6, k2tog, k4, m1, k1. P 1 row.

Next: skpo, k4, k2tog, k4, m1, k1. (12 sts) P 1 row.

Next: skpo, k10. (11 sts) P 1 row.

Next: skpo, k7, k2tog. (9 sts) P 1 row.

Next: skpo, k5, k2tog. (7 sts)

Next: p2tog, p3, p2tog tbl. (5 sts)

Cast off all sts.

With wrong side facing you, sew left-hand slanted edge of MC along the line where CC changes to MC. This makes a hollow cone-shape along the top of the wing, with the wide end open. Stuff this cone shape lightly (this helps hold wing out from body). Crochet with MC along outside edge of wing.

Left Wing

Knit wing with pair of 4 mm needles.

Cast on 43 sts with CC.

K 3 rows in garter stitch.

Next: k18, k2tog, PM, k9, k2tog, PM, k9, k2tog, k1. (40 sts) P 1 row.

Next: [k to last 2 sts before M, k2tog] twice, k to last 3 sts, k2tog, k1. P 1 row.

Repeat last 2 rows until 13 sts remain.

Break off CC, start next row with MC.

Next: k1, m1, k4, skpo, k6. P 1 row.

Next: k1, m1, k4, skpo, k4, k2tog. (12 sts) P 1 row.

Next: k10, k2tog. (11 sts) P 1 row.

Next: skpo, k7, k2tog. (9 sts) P 1 row.

Next: skpo, k5, k2tog. (7 sts)

Next: p2tog, p3, p2tog tbl. (5 sts)

Cast off all sts.

With wrong side facing you, sew right-hand slanted edge of MC along the line where CC changes to MC. This makes a hollow cone-shape along the top of the wing, with the wide end open. Stuff this cone shape lightly (this helps hold wing out from body). Crochet with MC along outside edge of wing – this helps wing to stop curling (you can also steam block the wing flat if you used a natural fiber).

Ears (make 2)

Knit ears with pair of 4 mm needles.

Cast on 10 sts with MC. K 1 row.

Next: k1, skpo, k6, m1, k1. K 1 row.

Repeat last 2 rows.

Next: k1, skpo, k to end. K 1 row.

Repeat last 2 rows 4 times (6 sts)

Next: k1, skpo, k2tog, k1. (4 sts) K 1 row.

Next: k1, skpo, k1.

Break off yarn, thread end through remaining stitches and pull tight to gather. Secure yarn end.

Finishing

Sew button eyes in place (or embroider eyes with black yarn if the toy is for a very young child). With length of yarn, embroider nose and mouth. Sew cast-on edge of ears in place on head, with slanted sides facing outwards. Sew head securely to open neck edge of body. Sew wings to body: sew open end of cone shapes to shoulders, then stitch inside edges of wings down the sides of the body, ending near the ankle.

JACK O'LANTERN

Materials

15 g worsted weight yarn in orange (O), small amount of worsted weight yarn in green (G), small amount of black yarn, stuffing, set of four 4 mm dpns, darning needle.

Measurements

7-10 cm (3-4") tall, 23 cm (9") around

Gauge

22 sts and 32 rows per 10 cm (4")

Cast on 9 sts with O, distribute between needles (3 sts per needle). K 1 round.
Next: [k1, m1] around. (18 sts)
K 1 round.
Next: [k1, m1] around. (36 sts)

Next: [k3, p1] around for 3 rounds.
Next: [k2, m1, k1, p1] 9 times. (45 sts)
Next: [k4, p1] around for 12-18 rounds, depending on how tall you want the pumpkin.
Next: [k1, k2tog, k1, p1] 9 times. (36 sts)
Next: [k3, p1] around for 3 rounds.
Next: [k2tog] around. (18 sts)
Break off O yarn and start next round with G. K 1 round.

Sew up hole in bottom and stuff pumpkin now.

Next: [k2tog] 9 times. (9 sts)
K 6 rounds, or until stem is as long as you want.
Break off yarn, thread end through sts and pull tight to gather. Secure yarn end.

Using G yarn, you can make a couple of stitches between pumpkin top and bottom, and snug them a bit to give the pumpkin a flat bottom.

Embroider face onto pumpkin with black yarn.

• •

OWL

Materials

35 g of worsted weight yarn in main colour (MC), 15 g of worsted weight yarn in contrasting colour (CC), 10 g of worsted weight yarn in yellow (Y), two 8 mm black buttons or safety eyes, stuffing, pair of 4 mm (US size 6) knitting needles, tapestry needle.

Measurements

18 cm (7") tall

Gauge

22 sts and 32 rows to 10 cm (4")

Feet (make 2)

Cast on 10 sts with Y yarn. P 1 row.

Next: k1, [m1, k1] to end. (19 sts)
P 1 row.
Next: k2, m1, k6, m1, k3, m1, k6, m1, k2. (23 sts)
Work 3 rows in st st.
Next: k6, [skpo] twice, k3, [k2tog] twice, k6.
Next: p4, [p2tog] twice, p3, [p2tog tbl] twice, p4.
Next: k6, s1, k2tog, psso, k6. (13 sts)
P 1 row.
Next: k1, [k2tog] across. (7 sts)

Break off yarn. Thread end through remaining stitches, pull tight and secure. Gather together cast-on sts, then sew back foot seam, leaving an opening. Stuff and then close opening. Use and extra length of yarn to make stitches to define the toes.

OWL
WITH A BABY

Body Back

Begin at neck edge.

Cast on 12 sts with MC. P 1 row.

Next: [k2, m1, k2] 3 times. (15 sts)
Work 5 rows in st st.

Next: k2, m1, k11, m1, k2. (17 sts)
Work 9 rows in st st.

Next: k5, m1, k1, m1, k5, m1, k1, m1,
 k5. (21 sts)
Work 9 rows in st st.

Next: k1, [k2tog] to end. (11 sts) P 1 row.

Next: k3, [k2tog] 3 times, k2. (8 sts)
Cast off all sts.

Body Front

Begin at neck edge.

Cast on 12 sts with MC. P 1 row.

Next: [k2, m1, k2] 3 times. (15 sts)
 P 1 row.
Break off MC, start next row with CC.
Work 4 rows in st st.

Next: k7, m1, k1, m1, k7. (17 sts)
Work 5 rows in st st.

Next: k7, m1, k3, m1, k7. (19 sts)
Work 5 rows in st st.

Next: k6, skpo, k3, k2tog, k6. (17 sts)
Work 3 rows in st st.

Next: k5, skpo, k3, k2tog, k5. (15 sts)
Work 3 rows in st st.

Next: k1, [k2tog] to end. (8 sts)
Cast off all sts.

Sew back to front along side and bottom
seams, leaving neck edge open. Stuff
body.

Right wing

Cast on 7 sts with MC. P 1 row.

Next: k1, [m1, k1] to end. P 1 row.
 (13 sts)

Next: k1, [p1, k1] across. P 1 row.

Next: skpo, k1, [p1, k1] across. P 1 row.

Next: skpo, [p1, k1] across. P 1 row.
Repeat these last 4 rows 5 times. (3 sts)

Break off yarn. Thread end through remaining stitches, pull tight and secure.

Left wing

Cast on 7 stitches with MC. P 1 row.

Next: k1, [m1, k1] to end. P 1 row.
 (13 sts)

Next: k1, [p1, k1] across. P 1 row.

Next: k1, [p1, k1] to last 2 sts, k2tog.
 P 1 row.

Next: [k1, p1] to last 2 sts, k2tog.
 P 1 row.
Repeat these last 4 rows 5 times. (3 sts)

Break off yarn. Thread end through remaining stitches, pull tight and secure.

Head

Cast on 7 sts with MC. P 1 row.

Next: k1, [m1, k1] to end. (13 sts)
 P 1 row.

Next: k1, [m1, k1] to end. (25 sts)
Work 3 rows in st st.

Next: [k2, m1] 4 times, k9, [m1, k2]
 4 times. (33 sts)
Work 9 rows in st st.

Next: with CC k15, MC k3, CC k15.

Next: CC p16, MC p1, CC p16.
Knit rest of head with CC.

Next: k3, [k1, k2tog] 3 times, k9, [skpo,
 k1] 3 times, k3. (27 sts)
Work 3 rows in st st.

Next: k1, [k2tog] to end. (14 sts) P 1 row.

Next: [k2tog] to end. (7 sts)

Break off yarn. Thread end through remaining stitches, and pull tight to gather.
Attach safety eyes. Sew up seam, leaving
an opening. Stuff and close opening.

Tail

Cast on 11 sts with MC. P 1 row.

Next: k1, [p1, k1] across. P 1 row.

Next: skpo, k1, [p1, k1] 3 times, k2tog.
 (9 sts) P 1 row.

Next: skpo, [p1, k1] 2 times, p1, k2tog.
 (7 sts)
Cast off.

Finishing

Sew button eyes in place (or embroider eyes with black yarn if the toy is for a very young child). Embroider beak with yellow yarn. Ears are made by knotting a length of yarn through a couple of sts on head, then trimming to desired length. Sew head securely to open neck edge of body. Add spots to body front with MC using duplicate stitch technique. Sew top edge of wings at shoulder position on the body. Sew feet securely in place. Sew tail to owl's bum.

BABY OWL

Materials

20 g of fuzzy worsted weight yarn, small amount of yellow yarn, two 8 mm black buttons or safety eyes, stuffing, pair of 4 mm (US size 6) knitting needles, tapestry needle, crochet hook.

Measurements

9 cm (3½") tall

Gauge

22 sts and 32 rows to 10 cm (4")

Start at bottom.

Cast on 18 sts. P 1 row.
Next: k2, [m1, k2] across. (26 sts) Work 9 rows in st st.

Next: k10, skpo, k2, k2tog, k10. (24 sts) P 1 row.
Next: [k1, skpo] 4 times, [k2tog, k1] 4 times. (16 sts) P 1 row.
Next: k2, [m1, k1] 5 times, k3, [m1, k1] 5 times, k1. (26 sts)
Work 7 rows in st st.
Next: k11, k2tog, skpo, k11. (24 sts) P 1 row.
Next: k5, skpo, k3, k2tog, skpo, k3, k2tog, k5. (20 sts)
Work 3 rows in st st.
Next: [k2tog] across. (10 sts)

Break off yarn, thread end through sts and pull tight to gather.

Attach safety eyes. Sew together center back seam to cast-on edge. Stuff toy, adding a bit of extra stuffing to the cheeks to make them stick out. Sew together cast-on (bottom) seam with fake grafting. Secure all yarn ends.

Sew on button eyes, or embroider with black yarn if toy is for a very young child. Embroider beak with yellow yarn. Make wings by knotting 15 cm (6") pieces of yarn at the shoulders, then trimming to right length. Add ears in same manner. For left foot, crochet a 6.5 cm (2½") cord, fold ends to center, then sew this spot to left side of the bottom seam. Repeat for right foot. Alternatively, embroider feet on body, or make feet from felt.

• •

Tip time!

A couple of tips for sewing. Gather together the cast-on stitches for the legs, arms, and head before sewing the straight seams. Use mattress stitch for the straight seams and for sewing the head to the body. For the top of the bunny's feet, use a stitch called "fake grafting" or "shoulder stitch."

Diagrams for stitches are easy to find on the web using any search-engine.

SPOOKY CAT
WITH A HOODED CAPE

CAT

Materials

50 g of black worsted weight yarn, small amount of pink yarn for embroidery, two 8 mm yellow buttons or safety eyes, stuffing, pair of 4 mm (US size 6) knitting needles, tapestry needle

Measurements

20 cm (8") tall

Gauge

22 sts and 32 rows per 10cm (4")

Legs (make 2)

Begin at sole.

Cast on 10 sts. P 1 row.
Next: k1, [m1, k1] to end. (19 sts)
 P 1 row.
Next: k4, [m1, k3] 5 times. (24 sts)
Work 3 rows in st st.
Next: k8, [skpo] twice, [k2tog] twice, k8. (20 sts)
Next: p6, [p2tog] twice, [p2tog tbl] twice, p6. (16 sts)
Next: k7, k2tog, k7. (15 sts)
Work 3 rows in st st.
Next: k2, m1, k11, m1, k2. (17 sts)
Work 11 rows in st st.
Next: k1, [k2tog] 8 times. (9 sts)

Break off yarn. Thread end through remaining stitches and pull tight to gather. Sew up sole and back leg seam, leaving an opening. Stuff and close opening.

Body

Begin at neck edge.

Cast on 16 sts. P 1 row.
Next: k1, [m1, k1] to end. (31 sts)
Work 3 rows in st st.
Next: k8, m1, k15, m1, k8. (33 sts)
Work 7 rows in st st.
Next: k15, m1, k3, m1, k15. (35 sts)
Work 3 rows in st st.
Next: k3, m1, k1, m1, k27, m1, k1, m1, k3. (39 sts) P 1 row.

Next: k16, skpo, k3, k2tog, k16. (37 sts)
Work 3 rows in st st.
Next: k15, skpo, k3, k2tog, k15. (35 sts)
Work 3 rows in st st.
Next: k1, [k2tog] to end. (18 sts) P 1 row.
Next: [k2tog] to end. (9 sts)

Break off yarn. Thread end through remaining stitches and pull tight to gather. Sew up back seam to neck edge (leaving neck edge open). Stuff body.

Right arm

Begin at paw tip.

Cast on 6 sts. P 1 row.
Next: k1, [m1, k1] to end. (11 sts)
 P 1 row.
Next: [k2, m1] twice, k3, [m1, k2] twice. (15 sts)
Work 3 rows in st st.
Next: k1, [skpo] twice, [k2tog] twice, k6. (11 sts)
Work 5 rows in st st.
Next: k5, [m1, k3] twice. (13 sts)
Work 9 rows in st st.
Next: k1, [k2tog] 6 times. (7 sts)

Break off yarn. Thread end through remaining stitches and pull tight to gather. Sew up seam, leaving an opening. Stuff and close opening.

Left arm

Begin at paw tip.

Cast on 6 sts. P 1 row.
Next: k1, [m1, k1] to end. (11 sts)
 P 1 row.
Next: [k2, m1] twice, k3, [m1, k2] twice. (15 sts)
Work 3 rows in st st.
Next: k6, [skpo] twice, [k2tog] twice, k1. (11 sts)
Work 5 rows in st st.
Next: k3, m1, k3, m1, k5. (13 sts)
Work 9 rows in st st.
Next: k1, [k2tog] 6 times. (7 sts)

Break off yarn. Thread end through remaining stitches and pull tight to gather. Sew up seam, leaving an opening. Stuff and close opening.

Head
Cast on 7 sts. P 1 row.
Next: k1, [m1, k1] to end. (13 sts)
  P 1 row.
Next: k1, [m1, k1] to end. (25 sts)
Work 3 rows in st st.
Next: [k2, m1] 4 times, k9, [m1, k2]
  4 times. (33 sts)
Work 11 rows in st st.
Next: k8, [k2tog] twice, k9, [skpo] twice,
  k8. (29 sts) P 1 row.
Next: k1, [k2tog] 6 times, k3, [skpo]
  6 times, k1. (17 sts)
Work 3 rows in st st.
Next: k1, [k2tog] to end. (9 sts)

Break off yarn. Thread end through re-maining stitches and pull tight to gather. Attach safety eyes to head now. Sew up seam, leaving an opening. Stuff and close opening. Make sure to put a bit of extra stuffing in the nose and cheeks to make them stick out.

Ears (make 2)
Cast on 9 sts. K 1 row.
Next: k1, skpo, k to end. K 1 row.
Repeat these 2 rows until 5 sts remain.
Next: k1, skpo, k2tog. K 1 row.

Break off yarn. Thread end through re-maining stitches, pull tight and secure end.

Tail
Cast on 9 sts.
Beginning with a P row, knit in st st until
  tail is about 12 cm (5") long.

Break off yarn. Thread end through stitches and pull tight to gather. Sew up seam.

Finishing
Sew button eyes in place (or embroider eyes with yarn if the toy is for a very young child). With length of yarn, em-broider nose and mouth with pink yarn. Sew cast-on edge of ears in place on head. Sew head securely to open neck edge of body. Thread a length of yarn through left arm about 1 cm (½") from top, thread yarn through body at shoulder position, then thread yarn through right arm. Thread yarn through body again, and then the left arm and pull tight. Repeat so yarn passes through each arm 3-4 times. Pull yarn tight so arms are secure, then fasten off yarn. Attach legs at lower edge of body in the same way as the arms. Sew tail to cat's bum.

HOODED CAPE

Materials
30 g of worsted weight yarn (MC), pair of 4.5 mm (US size 7) knitting needles, tapestry needle, crochet hook or ribbon

Measurements
19 cm (7½") long with hood, 22 cm (8½") wide

Gauge
20 sts and 26 rows to 10cm (4")

Cast on 45 sts.
Next 3 rows: k1, [p1, k1] across.
Next: [k1, p1] twice, k37, [p1, k1] twice.
Next: [k1, p1] twice, p37, [p1, k1] twice.
Repeat these last 2 rows 13 times.
Next: [k1, p1] twice, [k1, k2tog] 6 times, k1, [skpo, k1] 6 times, [p1, k1] twice. (33 sts)
Next: [k1, p1] twice, p25, [p1, k1] twice.
Next: [k1, p1] twice, [k2tog] 6 times, k1, [skpo] 6 times, [p1, k1] twice. (21 sts)
Next: [k1, p1] twice, p13, [p1, k1] twice.
Next: [k1, p1] twice, k13, [p1, k1] twice.
Next: [k1, p1] twice, p13, [p1, k1] twice.
Next: [k1, p1] twice, [k1, m1] 12 times, k1, [p1, k1] twice. (33 sts)
Next: [k1, p1] twice, p25, [p1, k1] twice.
Next: [k1, p1] twice, k25, [p1, k1] twice.
Repeat these last 2 rows 8 times.

Graft together top of hood, or cast off all sts and sew together top of hood. Make ties for the cape using ribbon or crochet-ing short cords.

ABBREVIATIONS

dpns = double-pointed needles

K or **k** = knit

k2tog = knit 2 together

k3tog = same as k2tog, but taking 3 sts

M = marker

m1 = make one by picking up loop between stitch just worked and next stitch, and knit into the back of this loop

P or **p** = purl

p2tog = purl 2 together

p2tog tbl = purl 2 together through back of loops

psso = pass slipped stitch over stitch just knit

s1 = slip one stitch

PM = place marker

skpo = slip 1, knit 1, pass slipped stitch over

st or **sts** = stitch or stitches

st st = stocking stitch

yo = yarn over